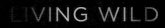

JELLYFISH

LIVING WILD

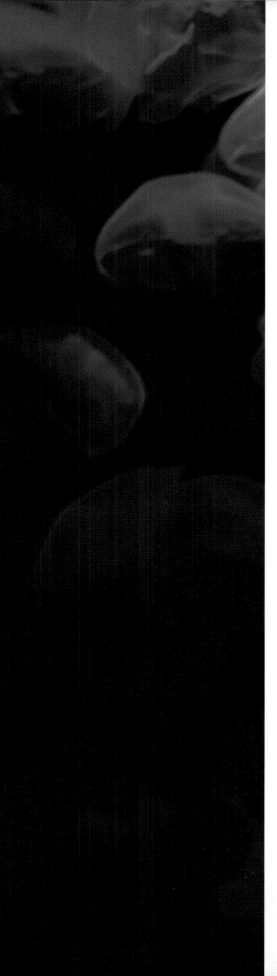

LIVING WILD

Published by Creative Education and Creative Paperbacks
P.O. Box 227, Mankato, Minnesota 56002
Creative Education and Creative Paperbacks are imprints of The Creative Company
www.thecreativecompany.us

Design and production by Mary Herrmann
Art direction by Rita Marshall
Printed in Malaysia

Photographs by Alamy (David Fleetham, Andrew Pearson), Corbis (Martin Almqvist/ Johnér Images; Paul Edmondson; Patricio Robles Gil/Sierra Madre/Minden Pictures; IC BOTHMA/epa; Thomas Kitchin & Victoria Hurst/All Canada Photos; Alex Mustard/2020VISION/Nature Picture Library; Scientifica, I/Visuals Unlimited; Norbert Wu/Minden Pictures; Norbert Wu/Science Faction), Creative Commons Wikimedia (Bella Galil, Nick Hobgood, André C. Morandini, NOAA/Monterey Bay Aquarium Research Institute, NOAA Ocean Explorer, Arnstein Rønning, Whinging Pom, Jonathan Wilkins), Dreamstime (Vitaliy Gerasimenko, Steve Lovegrove, Mav888, Uros Ravbar, Susan Sheldon, Bence Sibalin, Stephankerkhofs), NASA (NASA/Jeff Schmaltz/MODIS Land Rapid Response Team/NASA GSFC), Shutterstock (Greg Amptman, Mircea BEZERGHEANU, Chelsea Cameron, Suphatthra China, Ethan Daniels, Nicholas Peter Gavin Davies, Pichugin Dmitry, evantravels, Shane Gross, Michal Jablonski, stephan kerkhofs, MG image and design, Eugene Moerman, Allen McDavid Stoddard, Vilainecrevette). Image p. 33 © 2014 MBARI: This large jelly, Deepstaria enigmatica, was photographed about 1,050 meters below the ocean surface in Monterey Canyon. Inside its body is a pink parasitic amphipod.

Library of Congress Cataloging-in-Publication Data
Gish, Melissa.
Jellyfish / Melissa Gish.
p. cm. — (Living wild)
Includes bibliographical references and index.
Summary: A look at jellyfish, including their habitats, physical characteristics such as their bells, behaviors, relationships with humans, and their overabundance in the world today.
ISBN 978-1-60818-568-9 (hardcover)
ISBN 978-1-62832-169-2 (pbk)
1. Jellyfishes—Juvenile literature. I. Title. II. Series: Living wild.

QL377.S4G57 2015
593.5'3—dc23   2014028017

CCSS: RI.5.1, 2, 3, 8; RST.6-8.1, 2, 5, 6, 8; RH.6-8.3, 4, 5, 6, 7, 8

First Edition HC 9 8 7 6 5 4 3 2 1
First Edition PBK 9 8 7 6 5 4 3 2 1

CREATIVE EDUCATION • CREATIVE PAPERBACKS

JELLYFISH

Melissa Gish

In the clear, blue water of the Ogmore River,
a young compass jellyfish drifts upward.

The size of a dinner plate, it tucks its 4 arms and 24 tentacles into its bowl-shaped body.

In the clear, blue water of the Ogmore River, a young compass jellyfish drifts upward. The size of a dinner plate, it tucks its 4 arms and 24 tentacles into its bowl-shaped body. Around the fringe are 32 brown spots. Sixteen V-shaped lines radiate from a central brown spot on the top of the body to its fringes. It looks like just another clump of dead seaweed to unsuspecting prey. A shadow passes. The jelly responds instantly, extending its arms and tentacles, and pumps its body in pursuit. The shadow is a school of baby codfish. A curious fish nips at a wormlike tentacle, but the investigation turns deadly. The entangled fish struggles for just a moment as poison races from the tentacle into the fish's body. It will become the jellyfish's first meal of the day.

WHERE IN THE WORLD THEY LIVE

■ **Atolla Jellyfish**
Southern and
Pacific oceans

■ **Lion's Mane
Jellyfish**
Arctic and northern
Atlantic oceans

■ **Nomad Jellyfish**
Indian and Pacific
oceans

■ **Compass Jellyfish**
Mediterranean Sea
and South African
coasts

■ **Upside-down
Jellyfish**
Caribbean Sea
and southern Gulf
of Mexico

■ **Blue Jellyfish**
Irish and North
seas

■ **Helmet Jellyfish**
Norwegian fjords
and deep Atlantic
Ocean

The nearly 200 species in the Scyphozoa class of true
jellyfish inhabit both cold and tropical bodies of water
worldwide, from oceans and seas to rivers and swamps.
Many jellyfish frequent the waters along coasts, while other
jellies subsist only in the deepest regions of the sea. The
colored squares represent areas in which seven jellyfish
species are commonly found today.

J ellyfish were once considered one of the simplest creatures in the sea. Many species were generally grouped together simply because of their similar body structures. But now scientists are looking more closely at jellyfish and discovering many new and unique characteristics and behaviors. More than 10,000 species of jellyfish, jellyfish-like creatures, sea anemones, and corals are members of the phylum Cnidaria (*nid-AIR-ee-uh*). These animals are called cnidarians and are characterized by the use of tiny hooked, spear-like structures that shoot out of their bodies to capture prey. Cnidarians are divided into five separate classes in the subphylum Medusozoa. Some of these creatures are hydras and stalked jellyfish, which anchor themselves to rocks and other stationary surfaces, and others are cubozoas, or box jellyfish—the most deadly creatures on the planet. Of the more than 1,000 different species of medusozoans that have been discovered and named, the fewer than 200 in the class Scyphozoa (*SY-fuh-ZO-uh*) are considered true jellies. The word "scyphozoa" is derived from the Greek words *skyphos*, meaning "cup," and *zoa*, meaning "animal."

Unlike their free-floating jellyfish relatives, sea anemones typically remain anchored to one place.

The *Chrysaora* jellyfish genus is named for a character in Greek mythology, Chrysaor, whose name means "he who has a golden armament."

Stalked jellyfish move slowly by cartwheeling and gripping surfaces with their tentacles.

The term refers to the jellyfish's cup-shaped body. Despite the number of physical features they share, true jellies are distinguished from their relatives by differences in **DNA**.

When scientists first assigned the name jellyfish to these creatures in the 1700s, they did so because they gathered in groups like fish. They also resembled the jellied beef stock typically carried as food on ocean voyages. However, jellyfish are not fish, nor are they made of jelly. Most jellyfish can contract and flap their bodies, called bells, to push themselves forward. This pulsation is not true swimming. For this reason, jellyfish are considered zooplankton, a category of animals characterized by drifting in the water and being pushed along by currents. Jellyfish are invertebrates, which means they have no backbone. In fact, they have no skeletal structure at all. They have radial symmetry, which means that their body parts extend from a central point, like the spokes of a wheel. Their bodies are made up of about 98 percent water and feel like molded Jell-O®. Outside their ocean environments, they have no form and will lie as a gooey mass. The bell is made up of a jiggly substance called mesoglea sandwiched between two thin layers of

Not true jellyfish, box jellyfish can swim through the water at up to 4.6 miles (7.4 km) per hour.

Crown jellyfish are caught and used for food in Asian cuisine, their bells cut into strips and tossed with salads.

tissue. The inner tissue is called the gastrodermis, and the outer layer is called the epidermis. Jellyfish have cup- or umbrella-shaped bells. They have no heart and no head. Instead of a brain, jellyfish have a network of nerve cells called statocysts that help jellies sense direction and touch. Also, instead of eyes, some jellyfish have light-sensing organs called ocelli, which can detect the presence and absence of light.

Whether it is a rhizostome or not, any jellyfish stranded on shore is incapable of swimming back to the water.

Jellyfish have mouth-like structures, and the differences in how they eat further divide true jellyfish into three distinct groups: rhizostomes (*RYZ-uh-stomes*), coronates (*KOR-uh-nates*), and semaeostomes (*suh-MAY-uh-stomes*). The 92 species of rhizostomes have a bubble-shaped bell with 8 branching appendages called oral arms hanging down from the center of the bell. Each oral arm is covered with thousands of tiny holes. Rhizostomes prey on zooplankton that pass by the arms and become entangled. The oral arms then absorb the prey through the holes— like thousands of tiny mouths. The 47 species of coronates, commonly called crown jellies, have a deep groove running around the bell, which gives them their crown shape. Numerous flaps called lappets extend upward from

Compass jellyfish have both male and female organs but become either fully male or fully female to reproduce.

the edge of the bell. Lappets help tentacles nab passing prey such as **larval** fish, small shrimp, and **amphipods**. They then bend downward and push the prey into the orifice, a mouth-like opening beneath the bell. Inside the orifice is a space called the gastrovascular cavity, which serves as both stomach and intestine. Food is taken into the cavity, dissolved, and digested, and then waste material comes out. Semaeostomes are what most people visualize when they think of jellyfish. About 50 species have been identified. Their bells are ruffled, with four frilly oral arms hanging from the center. Numerous tentacles—reaching more than 100 feet (30.5 m) in some species—flow from the edge of the bell. When prey gets tangled in their tentacles or oral arms, semaeostomes flex these appendages to work the prey upward to the orifice.

Jellyfish are carnivores, meaning they eat other animals. They use their oral arms and tentacles for both capturing prey and defending themselves. The tentacles are covered with millions of sensitive hairs. The base of each hair is attached to a tiny needle-like projection called a nematocyst, which is coiled inside a pocket within the tentacle. Only the world's most powerful

The egg-yolk jellyfish's mild sting does not harm cleaner fish that seek out scraps of the jelly's smaller meals.

Each tentacle of the deadly sea wasp contains up to 5,000 nematocysts for pumping venom into its victims.

microscopes can detect nematocysts, which are about half the width of a human hair. The slightest pressure on a hair causes the corresponding nematocyst to shoot out and pierce the flesh of whatever creature touched it. The release of a nematocyst happens with amazing speed— in just 600 nanoseconds, which is 6 ten-millionths of a second. That is 100 times faster than a bullet travels down the barrel of a rifle. The **venomous** nematocysts almost instantly **paralyze** the jellyfish's victim. Jellies of all sizes stun prey in this way. Small jellies capture microscopic organisms, and large jellies catch fish, shrimp, and even other jellyfish. Some jellies have mild venom, but others have extremely powerful venom.

Some jellyfish relatives are deadly to humans. The sea wasp, a kind of box jellyfish, is the most venomous animal on the planet. With 60 tentacles trailing up to 10 feet (3 m) in length, this basketball-sized creature carries enough toxin in its body to kill 60 adults. While an **antivenom** exists, most people stung by sea wasps usually do not get the chance to use it—the victim's heart can shut down in two to three minutes. More than 100 people, mostly in Australia, have been killed by sea wasps.

True jellyfish are not nearly as dangerous to humans. While their stings can be painful, most jellies are not venomous enough to paralyze a human. Some people have allergic reactions to jellyfish toxins and become very sick, though. Skin cells can be permanently damaged by the venom, leaving victims with deep scars. People can encounter jellyfish in every ocean on Earth. These creatures float in shallow lagoons and drift through the deepest trenches. They exist in warm tropical waters as well as icy Arctic seas. Jellyfish have **adapted** to life in all the world's marine habitats.

Signs posted on beaches in Thailand warn of the potential for encountering box jellyfish in coastal waters.

Vinegar will deactivate jellyfish toxins on human skin, though it does nothing for toxins already in the bloodstream.

Palau's Jellyfish Lake in the Pacific Islands is home to millions of golden jellyfish that follow the sun.

BLOOMING JELLYFISH

Most jellyfish live no longer than a year, but a few species, including the cold-water helmet jelly, can live for 30 years. Predators take most jellies before they can even mature. Many kinds of fish, including sharks, sunfish, and tuna, will bite off chunks of jellyfish bells, which contain no venom. Some animals, such as sea turtles, are immune to jellyfish venom and will eat the entire animal. Leatherback sea turtles feed almost exclusively on jellyfish and can dive more than 1,000 feet (305 m) to hunt deep-sea jellies.

But the jellyfish's greatest threat comes from other jellyfish. Although a jellyfish will not kill members of its own kind, it will kill and eat different jellyfish species. Because jellyfish cannot swim, they cannot easily escape predators. Likewise, they cannot quickly chase prey. When two jellyfish drift into one another, the larger of the two will usually devour the smaller one.

Other sea creatures have relationships with jellyfish— some beneficial to the jellies and some harmful. Some species of amphipods are like little zombies. They can latch on to sea creatures and eat their flesh. In large

Bat stars, starfish relatives found in shallow waters from Alaska to Mexico, feed on jellyfish that drift near rocks.

A jellyfish relative as deadly as the sea wasp is Australia's Irukandji jelly, which is about the size of one M&M® candy.

A jellyfish polyp may feed on zooplankton or stingless jellyfish, which are defenseless in its tentacles.

enough numbers, these **parasites** can cause illness and even death. Jellyfish may fall victim to parasitic amphipods, but other animals, such as juvenile graceful rock crabs, like to eat these pests. Graceful rock crabs often hitch a ride on jellyfish to feed on the amphipods.

Because jellyfish drift with currents, they usually spend their entire lives in close proximity with one another, maturing about the same time. A jellyfish's reproductive organs, called gonads, depend on climate and sunlight to mature. When the time is right, all the jellyfish in a group, called a swarm, participate in reproduction.

Jellyfish do not choose mates. In some species, such as the cannonball jelly, the male shoots sperm out of his orifice toward the orifice of the nearest female, who catches the material. Once her eggs are fertilized, she expels them from her orifice. Most other jellyfish simply rely on luck to reproduce. Males release sperm, and females release eggs at the same time. If the sperm and eggs happen to drift into each other within a few hours, new jellyfish will be formed. For most species, this marks the end of their life cycle. After reproducing, they die.

Eggs that are fertilized, called planulae, are the first stage of the jellyfish's life cycle. They float for a while and then fall to the seafloor, where they anchor themselves to a rock or other stationary surface. Each planula develops into a minuscule organism with a trunk and a number of arms that grow into tiny tentacles. At this stage, it is called a polyp. The polyp is usually colorless. Its tentacles have nematocysts that spear anything that floats by and then curl downward to shove the food into an orifice in the center of the trunk. The polyp feeds for several weeks, growing to just 0.1 inch (2.5 mm) tall. After storing up enough energy, the polyp's tentacles shrink, and the

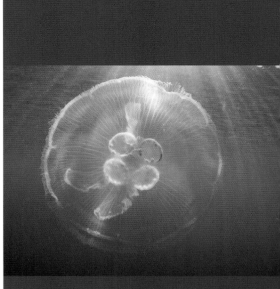

The moon jelly's digestive and reproductive organs are visible in the center of its transparent body.

The "pink meanie" feeds on moon jellies, which it traps in its 70-foot-long (21.3 m) tentacles.

At less than 0.75 inch (19.1 mm) in diameter, the tropical thimble jellyfish is one of the smallest true jellies.

trunk transforms into a segmented column. This form of a jelly is called a strobila. The segments then form into thin plates. When enough plates have stacked together, the strobila begins to contract, squeezing off each plate. This process is called strobilation, and these plates, called ephyra, are baby jellyfish. Each strobila's ephyra is a clone—an exact copy of all the other ephyra that developed from that strobila. The ephyra reach the adult jellyfish stage, called medusa, within several weeks or several months of strobilation, depending on the species.

But the reproductive process is not yet over. After releasing its plates, the strobila can shrink and regrow its tentacles, becoming a polyp once more. From this point, it can start the whole process of strobilation over again, or it can clone itself, creating another polyp. To do this, a mass of cells forms on the polyp's trunk. This mass grows rather large and soon falls off. Then the cell mass anchors itself next to its sibling and grows into a polyp. This new polyp can then strobilate, clone itself, or do both. The jellyfish's reproductive process allows for millions of jellyfish to be created in a single season. Many young jellies get eaten, but others survive. When hoards of jellies

Moon jellies can easily reproduce and gather in waters that do not support much other sea life.

A 2014 University of Washington (Seattle) study suggests that comb jellies may be one of Earth's first animals.

reproduce and number in the hundreds of thousands, the event is called a jellyfish bloom.

Such blooms can light up swaths of otherwise dark ocean on moonless nights. This is possible because about half of all jellyfish species have bioluminescent properties—their bodies can give off light. The jellyfish's body contains the chemicals luciferin (a pigment) and luciferase (an enzyme). When luciferin reacts with oxygen, luciferase speeds up the reaction, and the result is a protein that creates blue light. Jellyfish are highly sensitive to changes in their environment, so a temperature change, touch, or even the pressure of a wave as a fish passes by can trigger the reaction. Some species of jelly have an additional protein that scientists call GFP, which turns the blue light green. Depending on the species, a jellyfish's bioluminescence may begin as early as the egg stage or as late as when it reaches maturity.

A jellyfish relative with stunning bioluminescent abilities is the comb jelly. Most of the approximately 150 species exist in the deep sea. Similar to jellyfish, comb jellies are bell-shaped and have a mesoglea sandwiched between two layers of tissue. However, they can swim using cilia, which are rows of fine hairlike projections that wave back and forth like tiny oars, propelling the comb jellies in any direction. Like bioluminescent jellyfish, many comb jellies glow only blue or green. The moving cilia on some comb jellies scatter light, causing a rainbow of colors to race up and down the animal's body and, in some cases, along the tentacles. Unlike jellyfish, the comb jelly's tentacles do not sting. Instead, the lights attract prey, which get trapped on sticky cells called colloblasts that cover the tentacles.

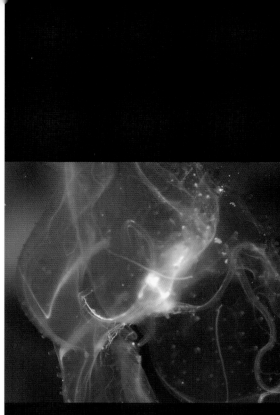

The venomous warty sea wasp lives in the Indian Ocean, where it displays its bioluminescent qualities.

The African freshwater jellyfish is featured in numerous cave drawings located in Algeria's Tassili n'Ajjer National Park.

JOYS OF JELLYFISH

The mysterious nature of jellyfish has been a source of fascination and folklore since the first human **cultures** ventured into the seas. However, well-preserved early representations of jellyfish, particularly in prehistoric artwork, are few and far between. While exploring the southern coast of France in 1985, professional diver Henri Cosquer discovered an entrance to an underwater tunnel at the foot of a high, jagged cliff. He made several trips to the site, each time traveling farther into the tunnel. Then, in 1991, after swimming more than 500 feet (152 m) through the tunnel, Cosquer emerged in a huge cave whose floor rose above sea level. The walls of the cave were covered with dozens of paintings and carvings of animals such as bison, antelope, horses, seals, seabirds, and jellyfish. He shared his discovery with **archaeologists** who determined that the artwork was made about 20,000 years ago. A subsequent expedition uncovered a deeper cave with even older artwork dating to 27,000 B.C. At this time in Earth's history, sea levels were lower, so the caves would not have been underwater.

Upside-down jellyfish typically group together in warm coastal swamps and seagrass beds.

Carrier crabs are so named because they carry upside-down jellyfish on their backs for protection.

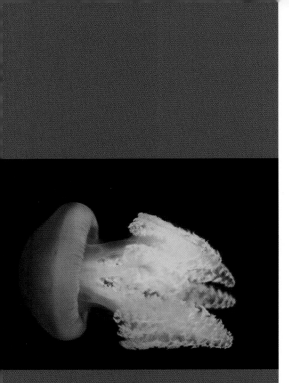

The jelly blubber is commonly found in Australian estuaries, places where ocean tides touch the mouths of rivers.

The Sahara Desert may seem an improbable place to find jellyfish, but 10,000 years ago, a freshwater jellyfish thrived there. In the language of the Berbers, an ethnic group native to North Africa, the name Tassili n'Ajjer means "Plateau of the Rivers." It was in this part of southeastern Algeria that European explorers discovered some of the finest and most abundant prehistoric rock art in 1933. When the art was made, about 10,000 years ago, this region of the Sahara Desert was a lush grassland with streams and lakes. And in these prehistoric lakes, as in most lakes in Africa today, lived the tiny African freshwater jellyfish. Though not a true jellyfish, this colorless creature resembles a moon jelly and is featured in some of the more than 15,000 drawings at Tassili n'Ajjer.

In 1891, Joseph Bradshaw, a rancher from the Kimberley region of Australia, happened upon some rocky outcroppings covered in prehistoric **Aboriginal** artwork. Called the Bradshaw Paintings today, these works date from between 26,500 and 20,000 years ago. Photographer and amateur archaeologist Grahame Walsh spent 30 years photographing and cataloging the images, which include representations of mostly humans but also

many animals—including jellyfish. Upon Walsh's death in 2007, more than 1.5 million images from the site had been recorded. In none of the world's rock art that includes jellyfish are there any clues as to how prehistoric people felt about jellyfish. Did they eat jellyfish? Fear them? Worship them? Jellyfish are rare amongst the many animals depicted in rock art, so archaeologists are left to wonder about their place in prehistoric human culture.

In modern times, people grew to hate jellyfish. A story was told in Iceland about how Jesus Christ and Saint Peter walked along the seashore one day and spat into the water. From this, halibut and lumpfish, important foods for Icelanders, were created. Then the devil walked along the seashore and spat into the water. This created the

SUMMER FRESHNESS

The sky is like a blue jellyfish.

And all around are fields, rolling meadows—

Peaceful world, you great mousetrap,

Would that I might finally escape from you ... O if I had wings—

One plays dice. Guzzles. Chatters about future countries.

Each person puts in his own two cents.

The earth is a succulent Sunday roast,

Nicely dunked into a sweet sun-sauce.

If only there were a wind ... that ripped

The gentle world with iron claws. That would amuse me.

But if a storm comes ... It would shred

The lovely blue eternal sky into a thousand pieces.

by Alfred Lichtenstein (1889–1914)

detestable jellyfish. A superstition born in Canada's Nova Scotia says that touching a jellyfish will cause warts. In "The Adventure of the Lion's Mane," a short story written by Scotsman Sir Arthur Conan Doyle in 1926, the famous detective Sherlock Holmes solves a murder mystery by deducing that the victim was killed by a lethal dose of lion's mane jellyfish venom.

Today, many experts agree that jellyfish are simply misunderstood. In 2012, an underwater camera used to monitor an oil-drilling rig in the Atlantic Ocean caught about six minutes of footage that caused a major stir on the Internet. A huge sheet-like object floating and swirling in front of the camera was nicknamed the "Cascade Creature," and when the video was uploaded to YouTube, millions of people viewed, shared, and commented on it. They speculated about what it could be, with ideas ranging from a giant plastic bag or a fishing net to an alien deep-sea creature. After about a month, officials from California's Monterey Bay Aquarium Research Institute (MBARI) concluded it could be *Deepstaria enigmatica*, a true jellyfish whose name means "mystery of the depths." The species' bell is only about two feet (61 cm) wide, but its thin

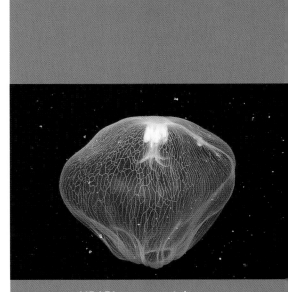

MBARI uses remotely operated vehicles (ROVs) to study deep-sea creatures such as Deepstaria enigmatica.

The egg-yolk jellyfish's venom is so mild that small crustaceans and amphipods often steal food from its oral arms.

structure sometimes flows like a sheet in the water, making the animal appear larger.

Perhaps the unique shapes, colors, sizes, and graceful movements of jellyfish all contribute to making them popular attractions at zoos and aquariums around the world. Many jellyfish exhibits travel from place to place. During its summer 2013 *Jelly Invasion* exhibit, the Vancouver Aquarium operated a live webcam for visitors to their website. Other aquariums such as the New England Aquarium in Boston and the Monterey Bay Aquarium keep permanent jellyfish exhibits. The largest jellyfish exhibit in the world is at Kamo Aquarium in Japan. About to close its doors because it was losing visitors and money, the aquarium came back to life when coral containing jellyfish polyps was put into a tank to replace a dead coral. The baby jellyfish that soon developed became so popular with visitors that the aquarium was able to stay open and eventually add hundreds more jellyfish (representing more than 35 species) to its underground exhibit area.

Jellyfish are also growing in popularity among home aquarium hobbyists. Moon jellies are the most common

jellyfish sold in pet stores. However, experts caution that the decision to keep jellyfish should not be made lightly. Jellyfish require extensive care. Water temperature, **salinity**, and chemical balance must be regulated daily. Jellyfish sold in so-called easy jellyfish kits often die within weeks. They need to be fed three times a day and housed in tanks without corners so they do not damage their fragile bodies. The water must continuously flow in a circular pattern to help jellies collect their food. Unlike a goldfish or a guppy, a jellyfish does not make a carefree pet. An easy way to interact with jellyfish, however, is by playing games with them—computer games, that is. SpongeBob SquarePants offers two free games on the Nickelodeon website: *Jellyfish Jumble* and *Jellyfish Shuffleboard*.

Pacific sea nettles are among the few jellyfish species to thrive in captivity, making them aquarium attractions.

Located in the Canadian Rockies, the 492-foot-thick (150 m) Burgess Shale has provided researchers with more than 60,000 fossils.

JELLYFISH INVASION

The oldest multi-organ animals on the planet, jellyfish have been around for more than 650 million years. But because jellyfish have soft bodies and contain mostly water, their fossil record is sparse. The best—and oldest—specimens found to date were discovered in Utah in 2007. Two **paleontologists** from the University of Utah uncovered jellyfish fossils that date to about 505 million years ago. Richard Jarrard and Susan Halgedahl, a husband-and-wife team, found 45 fossils of 4 different kinds of jellyfish. Most were only half an inch (1.3 cm) in diameter. However, the Utah fossils provided evidence of clearly shaped bells, tentacles, arms, and reproductive organs.

The fossils confirmed what scientists long suspected: jellyfish have changed very little since the first days of complex life on Earth. Prior to the Utah discovery, knowledge of early jellyfish was mostly limited to a series of discoveries that began in 1909 with American paleontologist Charles Doolittle Walcott. He found 505-million-year-old fossils of ctenophora, or comb jellies, in what is now the Burgess Shale Formation in

Jellyfish fossils, some older than 500 million years (such as that pictured), have been found in South Australia.

Even without tentacles, the ball-shaped nomad jellyfish is highly venomous, stinging victims with its fringed arms.

Unable to swim against tides, entire swarms of jellyfish may be beached by strong storm waves.

British Columbia's Yoho National Park. In 2007, experts from the University of Kansas and the National Science Foundation combined clues from the Burgess Shale comb jellies and the Utah fossils. They determined that either jellyfish **evolved** very quickly about 500 million years ago, or jellyfish have been on Earth as long as 700 million years, evolving slowly over time. The quest for more jellyfish fossils continues in order to determine which path ultimately led to the jellyfish we know today.

Jellyfish are some of the most resilient creatures on the planet. They have survived ice ages, violent geological phenomena that reshaped entire continents, and extinction events that wiped out thousands of species from the face of the earth. Today, **climate change** imperils the future of many forms of life—including humans. But along with a variety of human activities, climate change is turning the world's oceans into the best habitat that jellyfish have ever known. Jellyfish blooms are ever increasing. This may be good for jellyfish, but it spells disaster for every other living thing that depends on the health of the oceans.

In many cases, an overabundance of jellyfish has simply led to aggravation. In 1999, jellyfish were responsible

for turning out the lights across the northern half of the Philippines, leaving 40 million people—including the nation's president—thinking that the government had fallen victim to a hostile takeover. In truth, millions of jellyfish had been sucked into the cooling system of one of the island's main power stations, causing a power failure. To get the power back on, 50 truckloads of jellyfish first had to be removed from the system. In 2006, the USS *Ronald Reagan*, one of the United States Navy's largest and most advanced aircraft carriers, was left dead in the water by jellyfish. A jellyfish bloom blocked the seawater

Jellyfish unknowingly transported by ships have taken over the Black Sea, destroying a once-thriving fishery.

Founded in 1984, California's Monterey Bay Aquarium receives 1.8 million visitors each year and focuses on conservation.

needing to be pumped into the ship to cool its nuclear-powered engines. The engines had to be shut down while the system was cleared. These types of incidents happen around the world every year, from a 2008 shutdown of the Diablo Canyon nuclear power plant in California to recent shutdowns in Japan, Scotland, Sweden, and even Israel. In 2009, the Monterey Bay Aquarium's seawater intake system, which pumps fresh seawater into the exhibits, was clogged by millions of brown sea nettles—one of the most popular species on exhibit *inside* the aquarium.

Jellyfish blooms are also responsible for a series of major **ecological** disasters in recent decades. A salmon farm in the waters off Stewart Island (south of New Zealand) fell victim to jellyfish in 1998. Despite being penned in a bay, more than 56,000 salmon were killed by a swarm of moon jellyfish that had drifted into the bay. It wasn't the venom, which is mild in moon jellies, that killed the fish. Rather, the fish died when the jellies crowded the pen and suffocated the fish. A week later, the same thing happened at a salmon farm in southern Tasmania, killing 25,000 fish. Both farms have had other jellyfish invasions almost every year since then. Likewise, dozens of other fish farms around the world, from Norway to Chile, endure similar occurrences almost annually, with millions of fish lost to jellyfish stings and suffocation.

Scientists blame the rise in jellyfish blooms on several factors. Overfishing of jellyfish predators and competitors means that jellyfish can reproduce in vast numbers and survive unchecked. Fertilizers used in agriculture run

In 2003, scientists from the California Academy of Sciences were the first to collect a jellyfish called Big Red.

The rare *Thysanostoma loriferum* roams the open ocean trailing its rope-like arms tipped with needle-like projections.

into the ocean, where they feed algae. Algae blooms starve water of oxygen, creating dead zones with no animals. But jellyfish love these places, for they can feed on the algae undisturbed. By far, climate change is the greatest cause of jellyfish blooms. Rising ocean temperatures allow for more favorable conditions for jellyfish and their food sources, and increased rainfall raises river levels, causing more fresh water to flow into seas and oceans. Jellyfish easily adapt to such changes and move into areas from which they were previously absent. For example, many of Norway's **fjords** are now home to crown jellyfish—and only crown jellyfish. These jellies have destroyed many of Norway's fisheries, wiping out entire populations of crustaceans and fish by feeding on the eggs and larval forms of these animals.

While jellyfish are unique and fascinating creatures, their overabundance and invasion of fisheries is already spelling disaster for members of the ocean **food chain**. Researchers from the National Oceanographic and Atmospheric Administration (NOAA) as well as from Appalachian State University in North Carolina, Swansea University in Wales, James Cook University in Australia,

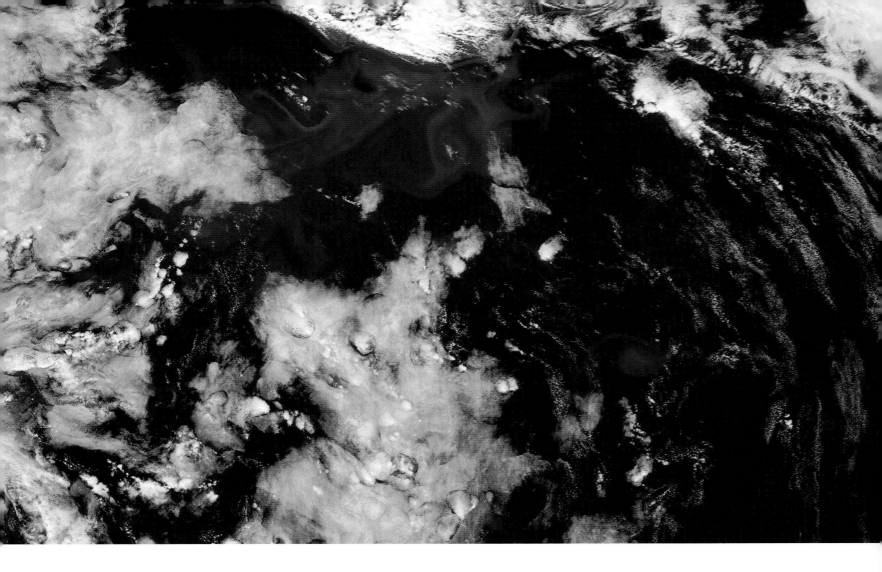

the Fisheries Research Agency in Japan, and a host of other organizations are conducting tracking projects to learn more about jellyfish. Tiny, vitamin-sized radio transmitters glued to jellyfish or fixed to belts tied around jellyfish bells send signals to receivers. The signals can be plotted on maps to track the animals' movements. Using this technology, researchers hope to learn where and why jellyfish blooms occur and how jelly populations can once again be balanced with other life in the sea.

A 2014 algae bloom in the North Atlantic was so far-reaching that it was visible from outer space.

ANIMAL TALE: JELLYFISH TURNS TO JELLY

In the Pacific Islands, sea creatures are important in mythology and traditional pourquoi, which are stories that explain how things came to be. Drawn from Japanese folklore, this story explains the unique characteristics of the jellyfish.

Long ago, Jellyfish had the longest legs, the shiniest scales, and the strongest shell of all the creatures in the sea. Jellyfish was magnificent, but he could never keep a secret.

One day, the Queen of the Sea awoke with a pain in her stomach. The doctors determined that she needed a new stomach, and only the stomach of Bear would do. The queen ordered Jellyfish to leave the water and use his long legs to run into the forest to find Bear. Jellyfish did so and brought Bear back to the sea.

The queen told Bear that everyone in the sea admired him and wished to give him a party. Bear was flattered and stepped into the water. Jellyfish laughed.

"Silly Bear," Jellyfish said. "Don't you know they are going to kill you and steal your stomach?"

With a roar, Bear leaped out of the water and ran back to the forest.

The Queen of the Sea was angry with Jellyfish. "You do not deserve your legs," she said. And she took them away, leaving Jellyfish with only limp tentacles.

This ordeal caused the queen to feel a sudden pain in her heart. The doctors determined that she needed a new heart, and only the heart of Blue Whale would do. The queen ordered Jellyfish to use his shell to dive deep in search of Blue Whale.

Jellyfish did so and returned with Blue Whale. The queen told Blue Whale that everyone in the sea admired him and wished to give him a party. Blue Whale blushed, but Jellyfish laughed.

"Silly Blue Whale," Jellyfish said. "Don't you know they are going to kill you and steal your heart?"

Blue Whale quickly dove beneath the waves, leaving the queen angrier than before. "Jellyfish!" she cried. "You do not deserve your shell!" And she took it away, leaving Jellyfish naked.

The queen's distress caused a pain behind her eyes. The doctors determined that she needed new eyes, and only the eyes of Albatross would do.

"Please give me one more chance," begged Jellyfish. "I will bring Albatross to you."

"Very well," the queen said. "This is your last chance." She ordered Jellyfish to float on the water so his beautiful scales would attract Albatross. Jellyfish did so and lured Albatross to the queen.

The queen told Albatross that everyone in the sea admired him and wished to give him a party. Albatross was thrilled. Jellyfish tried to hold back his laughter—but he could not.

"Silly Albatross," Jellyfish said. "Don't you know they are going to kill you and steal your eyes?"

Albatross immediately flew away. "You fool!" the queen screamed. "You do not deserve your shiny scales!" And she took them away, leaving Jellyfish with a slimy, see-through body.

The queen still feels great pain sometimes, which causes her to cough and shake, thus creating terrible undersea earthquakes and tidal waves. And to this day, Jellyfish remains tossed around at the mercy of the waves, for he has no legs, no shell, and no scales to protect him.

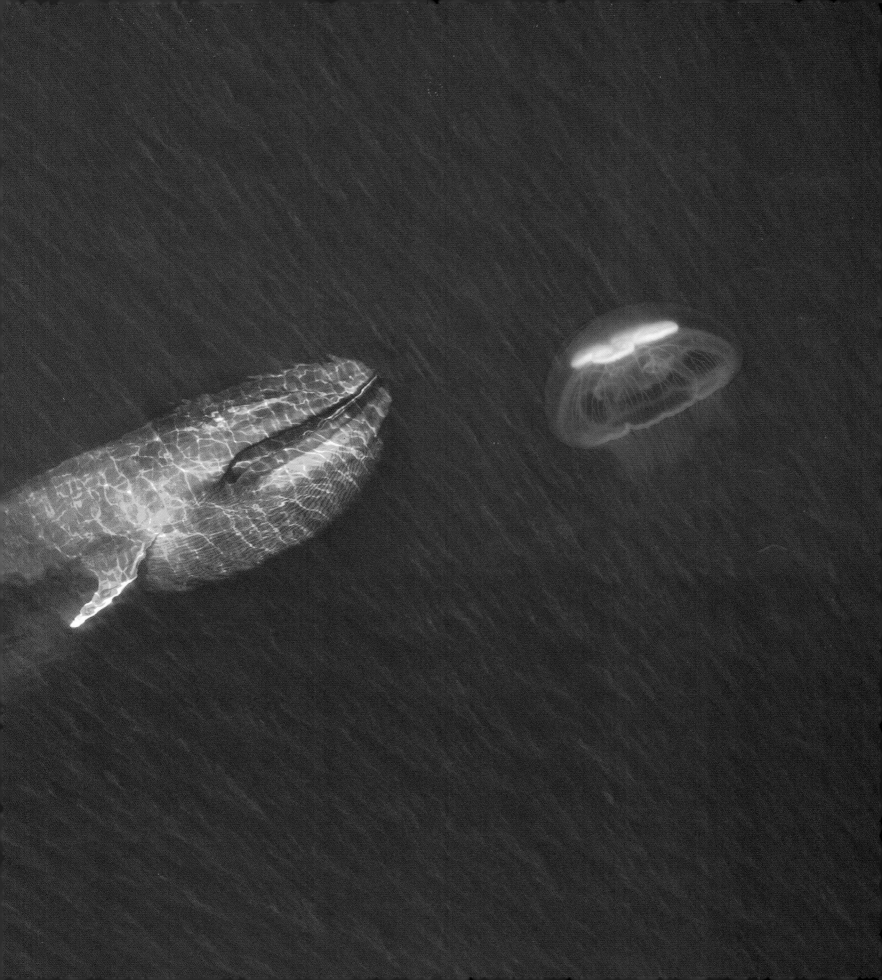

GLOSSARY

Aboriginal – of or relating to the Australian Aborigines, the people who inhabited Australia before the arrival of European settlers

adapted – changed to improve its chances of survival in its environment

amphipods – small, soft-bodied crustaceans with laterally compressed bodies

antivenom – a substance created to counteract the effects of a venom

archaeologists – people who study human history by examining ancient peoples and their artifacts

climate change – the gradual increase in Earth's temperature that causes changes in the planet's atmosphere, environments, and long-term weather conditions

cultures – particular groups in a society that share behaviors and characteristics that are accepted as normal by that group

DNA – deoxyribonucleic acid; a substance found in every living thing that determines the species and individual characteristics of that thing

ecological – having to do with the interdependence of organisms living together in an environment

evolved – gradually developed into a new form

fjords – narrow, deep inlets of the sea between high cliffs or slopes

food chain – a system in nature in which living things are dependent on each other for food

larval – of the newly hatched, often wormlike, form of many fish, crustaceans, and insects before they become adults

mythology – a collection of myths, or popular, traditional beliefs or stories that explain how something came to be or that are associated with a person or object

paleontologists – people who study fossils of animals, plants, and other organisms that existed long ago

paralyze – to produce a loss of muscle movement

parasites – animals or plants that live on or inside another living thing (called a host) while giving nothing back to the host; some parasites cause disease or even death

salinity – the amount of salt in water

venomous – capable of injecting poison by a sting or bite

SELECTED BIBLIOGRAPHY

Gershwin, Lisa-ann. *Stung!: On Jellyfish Blooms and the Future of the Ocean*. Chicago: University of Chicago Press, 2013.

National Geographic. "The Ocean: Photo Gallery; Jellyfish." http://ocean.nationalgeographic.com/ocean/photos/ocean-jellyfish/.

National Geographic Kids. "Animals: Jellyfish." http://kids.nationalgeographic.com/animals/jellyfish/.

Nouvian, Claire. *The Deep: Extraordinary Creatures of the Abyss*. Chicago: University of Chicago Press, 2007.

Piper, Ross. *Extraordinary Animals: An Encyclopedia of Curious and Unusual Animals*. Westport, Conn.: Greenwood, 2007.

Whitaker, J. David, Rachael King, and David Knott. "Sea Science: Jellyfish." South Carolina Department of Natural Resources. http://www.dnr.sc.gov/marine/pub/seascience/jellyfi.html.

Note: Every effort has been made to ensure that any websites listed above were active at the time of publication. However, because of the nature of the Internet, it is impossible to guarantee that these sites will remain active indefinitely or that their contents will not be altered.

The flower hat jelly is a non-deadly jellyfish relative found only in the western Pacific off the coast of Japan.

INDEX

atolla jellyfish 10

Big Red jellyfish 41

blue jellyfish 10

brown sea nettles 41

cannonball jellyfish 23

compass jellyfish 7, 8, 10, 16

cultural influences 11, 29–31, 33, 35, 44
    computer games 35
    folklore 29, 31, 33, 44
    Internet videos 33
    literature 33
    mythologies 11, 44
    prehistoric artwork 29, 30–31

Deepstaria enigmatica 33–34

egg-yolk jellyfish 34

habitats 7, 10, 12, 19, 26, 30, 33, 38, 42, 43
    estuaries 30
    fjords 10, 42
    lakes 30
    oceans 10, 12, 19, 26, 30, 33, 38, 42, 43
    rivers 7, 10, 30
    seas 10, 19, 42

helmet jellyfish 10, 21

jelly blubber 30

jellyfish blooms 26, 38–40, 41–42, 43
    causes of 41–42, 43
    ecological effects of 41, 42

life expectancy 21

lion's mane jellyfish 10, 33

moon jellyfish 23, 34, 41

movement 7, 8, 12, 19, 21, 22, 34, 41

nomad jellyfish 10, 37

physical characteristics 7, 8, 12, 15–16 18, 19, 21, 22, 23,
    24, 26–27, 33–34, 37, 41, 42, 43, 44
    arms 7, 8, 15, 16, 34, 37, 42
    bells 12, 15, 16, 21, 33–34, 37, 43
    bioluminescence 26–27
    lappets 15–16
    nematocysts 16, 18, 23
    orifices 16, 23
    reproductive organs 16, 22, 37

sensory organs 15
sizes 7, 23, 24, 34
tentacles 7, 8, 16, 23, 24, 37
venom 8, 18, 19, 21, 33, 34, 37, 41

"pink meanie" jellyfish 23

populations 38–39, 41, 42, 43

predators 21, 41
    fish 21
    jellyfish 21
    sea turtles 21
    sharks 21

prey 8, 11, 15, 16, 18, 19, 21, 23, 35, 42
    crustaceans 16, 18, 42
    fish 8, 16, 18, 42
    jellyfish 19
    zooplankton 15

relationships with humans 19, 31, 34–35, 38
    as pets 34–35

relatives 11, 12, 19, 21, 27, 30, 34, 37–38
    African freshwater jellyfish 30
    anemones 11
    box jellyfish 11, 19
    comb jellies 27, 37–38
    coral 11, 34
    Irukandji jellyfish 21

reproductive process 16, 22–24, 26, 27, 34
    eggs 23, 27
    ephyra stage 24, 34
    medusa stage 24
    polyp stage 23, 24, 34
    strobilation 24

scientific research 37–38, 42–43
    and fossils 37, 38
    tracking 43

Scyphozoa class 10, 11–12, 15–16, 24, 33, 42
    coronates 15–16, 42
    rhizostomes 15
    semaeostomes 15, 16

thimble jellyfish 24

Thysanostoma loriferum 42

upside-down jellyfish 10, 29

zoos and aquariums 33, 34, 40–41